Amazon Echo Dot 3rd Generation User Manual for Everyone

The Step by Step Guide to learning how to use Alexa, Troubleshoot the Echo Dot in 30 Minutes like a Master! 2019 Edition

By

Clayton M. Rines

Acknowledgments

This book could not have been written without the guidance and generosity of everyone I have come in contact with one way or another. Your influences are all over this book. Thank you.

DEDICATION

This book is dedicated to everyone seeking for knowledge out there.

Disclaimer

All the information contained in this book is purely for educational activities only. The writer does not assert the accuracy or wholesomeness of any info gotten from this book. The views contained within the pages of this material are those of the author in its entirety. The author/writer will not be held accountable or liable for any missing information, omissions or errors, damages, injuries, or any losses that may occur from the use of information gotten from this book.

Contents

CHAPTER ONE

AMAZON ECHO DOT 3RD GENERATION

UNLEASHING THE NEW AMAZON ECHO DOT 3RD GENERATION

Amazon has made a lot of improvements to their generation of Echo Dot with the introduction of the New Amazon Echo Dot 3rd Generation. Part of it is an improvement in the quality of sounds compared to other versions of the Echo Dot irrespective of the number of speakers. Apart from the sound quality amongst many other improvements, the third generation now looks bigger when compared to the previous generations.

FEATURES

i. The device look has been changed now having fabric placed around its sides located at the rounded corners, which gives it a much more attractive look.

ii. Amazon has also included four microphones that are placed at the back.

iii. An in-built speaker of 1.6 inches has also been added to this new generation unlike in previous generations which used to have the 1.1-inch speaker. This has resulted in the improvement of its sound quality with louder productivity and lesser distortion.

iv. Light indicators are also placed at the top to help you in knowing the status of your echo device such as when muted it will indicate a red light, but when it is on standby, it will show the blue color.

v. The buttons on the device are also minimal, having the volume up/down, mute button as well as the action button.

Like in the second generation, the third generation of the Amazon Echo dot might have been set up already by default. Therefore, the device might be ready for use with minimum setting up process needed. Nevertheless, previous generations will prompt you on how to go about the setting up process, which makes it a whole lot easy road to go.

CHAPTER TWO
THE AMAZON ECHO DOT SECOND GENERATION VS THE THIRD GENERATION

New Amazon Echo 3 is a much larger speaker, and the reason is that they want to make it a speaker instead of having a hockey puck that does voice commands. Another feature they changed is that on the new Amazon echo dot 3, it now uses a DC power supply. Instead of having a USB connector, you now have the DC input and also 12 watts power. Amazon echo dots do support 2.4 gigahertz for Wi-Fi as well as 5gb. The most significant increase in the new one is that it now supports AC Wi-Fi so that you can obtain a little bit more range on it.

For both of these speakers, you can add some custom colors, for example, the Echo dot 3 covering cloth is available in three different colors: charcoal, health grey, and stone. If you want to customize your echo, Amazon has some predetermined colors that you can buy, and then you slip this right inside of it. Another thing about Amazon Echo dot is that it has been out for a while so you can pair a variety of external accessories like speakers.

Now when both are plugged precisely at the same time, we can get to see how long they turn on and get it programmed to see if there are any hiccups or if one is better than the other. So install the Alexa app and follow the instructions. Once the device is ready for setup, follow the instructions in your Alexa app. The echo 3 connects to the service so much better; therefore, that is a plus.

The Amazon Echo 2 has the USB power supply, so you can easily add it to a car or any of the extra accessories. It has a smaller size, and it has seven microphones. When it comes to Amazon echo dot 3, you have a much better sound quality, it's slightly faster, but the downside is that it has four microphones and has that proprietary charging port which right off the bat. Below is some obvious comparison to note about the Amazon Echo dot of the 2nd and 3rd generation.

• The Amazon Echo Dot 3rd generation is made up of larger speakers, which are 1.6 inch, which makes it half an inch bigger compared to the second generation echo dots. This, in turn, makes it 25% larger and much taller when compared to that of the second generation.

• The new Amazon 3rd generation is made up of four microphones, unlike the second generation whose speakers are seven in number. Though, irrespective of the number of speakers, the sound quality of the third generation is better than those of the previous generations.

• Both the second and third generations of the Amazon echo dot have the same number of ports available in them, but in terms of power, the third generation comes with more power having fifteen watts, unlike the second generation which only has nine watts.

• Nevertheless, both the second and third generations of the Amazon echo dot share the same similarities having the same port configuration as well as having the same light ring on them.

Amazon Echo 3rd Generation versus the Google Home mini

Some time ago, Google one-upped Amazon by introducing a couple of different products one of which was the Google home mini smart speaker and was the new competitor to Amazon's echo dot specifically the second generation at the time. Amazon has been able to level the playing field with the introduction of the Amazon Echo dot of the third generation.

In terms of audio quality and video output, which was the big difference, the Google Home mini was way better than the previous generation of the echo dot; now they are pretty similar versus Google assistant.

Both of them are now covered with what they call acoustically transparent fabric to ensure that it doesn't bring an interfere with the audio coming out which comes out from the sides. In the Amazon Echo Dot Third generation, the sound comes out the top. If you're listening to the devices, they're going to sound a little bit different.

In terms of usability, buttons and tactile controls, I'm going to give the advantage to Amazon here because they have tactile controls that you can feel. Google's design is very minimalistic, it will sit in your home, and both of these would do anyways. With their multiple colors and finish choices, they would look great in any décor and will also match up very nicely. The micro USB power input is on the back of the Google Home Mini and on the end of the echo dot third-generation you've got proprietary power. They have the 3.5-millimeter stereo output, which is a very popular reason why people buy the Echo 3 to connect them to more powerful speakers.

They both connect to the bluetooth and WiFi so you can Bluetooth stream to the devices for both the Echo dot 3 and the Google Home mini. If you want to get sounds out of the

Google Home Mini, you can Bluetooth stream to other devices but again no 3.5-millimeter output.

You can also cast like chrome cast or cast several other devices. You can cast sounds from some of your gadgets straight to the Google speakers. Amazon is working on a cast-like service; it only works with Amazon music right now. Their audio output is very similar, about 85 to 90 decibels when in a serene room with no external noisenat high volumes.

Another essential comparison is when it comes to their voice response, which is what these things do, of course, they both do them comprehensively maybe both answer you equally anyways. If you are watching some movies or TV shows or something like that, the device can easily pick out your voice over that of the TV.

Also, you can now pair your echo dot along with stereo pairing which was only present in Google home max speakers. Pairing is now also available for the regular echo, the echo plus, and the third-generation echo dot to give you that excellent stereo separation, which is another advantage from Amazon. Amazon has done well-having lots of benefits with its lineup of devices that keep getting wider every single year.

CHAPTER THREE

ASSESSMENT OF OUR PRIVACY LEVEL WITH THE AMAZON ECHO DOT 3

First, what happens when you speak to your device? According to Amazon, when you talk to your device, a recording of what you asked is sent to Amazon's cloud where they process your requests and other information to respond to you.

Is your device always recording information? Amazon says, No! As a preset value, the gadget has been designed to respond only to your chosen wake word. The device reacts to the command word by identifying audio patterns that fits perfectly with the command word. No audio file is kept or relayed to the cloud storage only if your device picks up the wake word. Okay, that's good it's not always recording your conversations.

Another question you might ask yourself is: Can I review or delete my recordings? Sure, you can go through audio files linked to your account and erase those voice recordings sequentially or all at once by visiting the app or a link on their web page to see the recordings.

So if I can get rid of the recorded information it collects, but how are those recordings being used? Amazon makes use of your audio prints and other biodata, including those from other service providers to give you a response and continue to provide a pleasant experience for you. Your requests are associated with your Amazon account to allow you to review your voice recordings and access other Amazon services, such as Kindle books and audiobooks, and to provide you with a more personalized experience.

How does your voice do improves the process? According to Amazon, it helps your device become smarter every day. The more time you spend with your device, the more it gets use to you and your likes and preferences. For example, your requests are used to train the Amazon's speech recognition and natural language understanding systems.

Now, what about being hacked? In a Wired article, it shows that a group of hackers found a way to get into echo devices. Not that it was easy to do. But they did take apart an echo device and reprogram it to be able to access vulnerabilities in the web and the services.

Even if something is being recorded, now hackers have to hack into Amazon to get that recording. It sounds like a lot of work. Why not steal a bunch of credit card information instead. Now Amazon takes your security very seriously, which includes disallowing third-party installation on the devices, extensive security overviews, top notch software production processes and coding of information between you, the app and Amazon servers.

Like I said unless you're recording something sensitive and then hackers go-ahead to hack into your account to hear your recordings, the chances are pretty slim.

But to feel safer, you might want to take the initiative of protecting your devices.

• First, make sure to protect your network.

• Next, you can change the Wake word of your device.

•You can also strengthen your Amazon password which wouldn't be a bad idea anyway.

• From there you can delete old recordings, especially those with sensitive information but note that if you do delete those recordings, it will take away some of the personalized experience.

• Lastly, read third-party policies to see what they're allowed to do. But according to Amazon, those third parties are not going to be able to install any software on the device itself. Those third party skills are being stored in the cloud, unlike apps that you download onto your phone that are sitting right next to the personal information that is stored on your phone.

So, after all, I've read and learned I'm not too concerned about the privacy level of echo devices because:

• It has to hear the Wake word before it's going to store any of your information.

• It's just a voice that's going to and from the servers. Nothing's actually on the device

The most important thing is that there's too much value for Amazon to keep our trust and not violate it. They make their money off of selling products by us shopping on Amazon. Therefore, if our trust is broken, why are we going to shop there, that will affect them. Nevertheless, virtual assistants are going to become more commonplace.

CHAPTER FOUR

SETTING UP THE AMAZON ECHO DOT 3RD GENERATION

Before starting with the setup process, you are advised to make use of original accessories to get optimal performance, preferably accessories that were packed with your device at the point of purchase. Then you will need to follow all instructions as stated out by the Alexa app:

i. Get your Echo dot device plugged to get started and wait for Alexa to say "hello." This is the first two most important steps of setting up your Echo dot 3rd generation.

ii. Get your power adapter and plug one side to the wall while your power cord is then connected to the back. This will result in a blue right ring spinning around the top, and you will be greeted by Alexa, which will put you through on how to get the Setup process completed.

iii. You will need to get the Alexa app downloaded, which is very important for effective use of your Echo device.

iv. Once you have been able to download the Alexa app from the Amazon play store and Alexa is not prompting you, you will need to get on the Alexa app and click on the device's icon.

How to download Alexa app

• You need to download the Alexa app so it can be used to interact with your Echo device. The app can be gotten from the AppStore on the iPhone and Play store from an android device.

• Once you have obtained the Alexa app, you will then launch the app which will need you to log in to your Amazon account if you are doing this on the device for the first time.

• Afterward, you will need to get the echo dot device added by scrolling down and clicking on the house icon. Nevertheless, if you have gone through the process of setting up your Amazon devices before, the Alexa app will take you through the automatic set up process instead of having to click on the home icon at the bottom right-hand corner.

• The next step is to select your Echo device as well as Alexa and also, more importantly, make sure you are using a working Wi-Fi connection. Once you have chosen your Echo and Alexa, you will be prompted to get your Echo dot plugged to a power outlet. Once the Echo dot is connected, the blue light will turn to an orange light one minute after it must have been plugged after which you can go ahead and select continue.

• In a situation where you are having a problem getting your Echo dot connected automatically, you will be prompted to connect instead manually. Once this happens, go to the Wi-Fi or internet settings of your phone and click on "Amazon at TFN open," after which you click on connect to get connected manually.

• Once you are connected, go to the Alexa app where you will be prompted to continue with the Setup process of your Echo dot and click on continue.

• You will then be asked which Wi-Fi network you like to get connected to which is why you should have a working Wi-Fi already set up before this.

• Once the Wi-Fi network has been chosen, you will be prompted to wait while your Echo dot gets connected to the internet. This connection process might take a few minutes after which your device will be ready for use and then go ahead to click on continues.

CHAPTER FIVE

USEFUL TIPS AND TRICKS

How to pair a Bluetooth device to your Amazon Echo dot 3rd Generation

Get your Mobile device > Search for the Amazon Alexa app and open it > Go to the bottom right-hand corner of the Amazon Alexa app and click on a house icon that you will find there which will navigate you to the device's page > Click on all devices > Select the echo dot device that you will be pairing, which is your Amazon Echo Dot 3rd generation and click on it > Once you have clicked on the echo dot device, look out for where there are Bluetooth devices and click on it. It is to be noted that it will take a few seconds to get booted into your Bluetooth settings > If you haven't made use of any Bluetooth device before with your Echo dot 3rd generation, you will be prompted by the device that you haven't paired any device previously with it, and it is your first time of engaging in the Bluetooth pairing > Select the Pair a new device which will automatically start searching for a device to pair with. So before this, you must ensure that the Bluetooth device you will be pairing is in the pairing mode. If you are pairing your Mobile device, for example, you must ensure that it is in its pairing mode before selecting the Pair a new device option > Go back to your Amazon Alexa app, now that both the Bluetooth device and Echo dot are in the pairing mode, and the paired device will automatically pop up on the Amazon Alexa app > Click on the Bluetooth device once it pops up on the Alexa app then go-ahead to have it paired.

Once you can follow these steps correctly, you can be sure that your Bluetooth device must have been successfully paired with the Echo dot 3rd generation device which applies to all Bluetooth devices being paired with the Amazon Alexa app.

How to make use of the Smart Home Group with the Echo Dot 3rd Generation

Multiple devices can be controlled using the Smart home group that was introduced by Amazon by having the devices grouped so that you won't have to go through the stress of needing to keep track of all your devices as they come into your house. With this feature developed by Amazon, you will have all your devices placed into one.

The Amazon Echo dot 3rd generation can also be added as part of the devices in the group which comes in very handy because once you have the echo device placed in the group, you will get to use the Alexa voice assistant in performing different actions. You can easily dish out Alexa commands like saying stuff like, "Echo, turn on the light" and it will able to detect automatically that you are talking about the light. Therefore, if the Echo device is added to the office group, it will automatically turn on the light in the office groups, which gives you perfect control over the entire group. This will also apply to other things like media, music, etc.

To set up your Smart Homegroup, you will need to have a mobile device where the app will be downloaded for control.

Go to the top corner of the screen and click all devices. This will display a list of all devices that you must have installed on the app > Afterward, you will need to get groups created, such as a living room group, bedroom group, and the office group, and so on > Using the office group as an example, go to the top of the screen and tap the plus sign at the right-hand corner. Here you will be able to add a group, give it a name like in this example; we are naming the group "Office," then tap "Done," and "Next," afterward > After which you will go ahead and add devices, such as the Echo devices, so you make use of the voice assistant, you can also add the lamps in the office, etc., majorly all the devices you want to have control over > Once you have added your devices, tap on the "Save" option.

Once saved, you will now have an Office group with the echo device and office lights added which will give you control over all the lights in the office making use of simple commands such as "Echo, turn on the light," and all the lights in the office will go off. Like said earlier, this also applies to other features you might like to control with the Echo device such as speakers and anything you want to have control over using the simple voice commands.

How to Troubleshoot an Unresponsive Echo Dot

Sometimes, issues do arise where your device becomes irresponsive to commands. This is a common issue so it's nothing to be worried about as there are steps you can take to help you in countering matters like this.

To help solve this issue, consider the following steps:

• Make sure you are using the specified power adaptor because other adaptors might not have the capacity required for your device or they might not be able to provide the power needed for your Echo dot.

• Once you have been able to check with your power adaptor, test to see if the echo dot answers any request given to it by clicking on the action button.

• If the echo dot is closer to a speaker via Bluetooth, there is every possibility it will be able to respond to commands to help solve the issue. Ensure that the Echo dot device is at least three feet away from the speaker.

• Also, make sure that no external speaker is interfering with your requests as this may make it hard for the Echo dot to listen to your requests and other wake words. Therefore it is vital to make sure the Echo dot is placed far from external speakers.

• Noise can also make your Echo dot device unresponsive. Therefore, avoid noise whenever you speak to the echo dot, so it doesn't interfere with your request, and the Echo dot can listen to you.

• Another thing to look out for is object or wall interference as this might make it difficult for the Echo dot to hear from you. Make sure your echo dot device is about 20 centimeters away from objects or walls in your offices or home.

How to De-register and factory reset an Amazon Echo Dot 3rd Generation

There are situations you might decide to give away or sell your Echo dot device. When this happens, there will be a need to get it de-register and perform a factory reset on it. There are several altenate paths that you can take to achieve the desired goal, with the easiest one being the use of the Alexa app. The process will help in deactivating your device from Amazon account, and the device will go back to the starting mode.

It is essential to make sure you have your Amazon Echo Dot connected to a working internet via a wireless network, preferably the network you used in opening or setting up the device in the first place.

Using the Amazon Alexa app for the iOS device, you are required to take the following steps:

Open the Alexa app > Scroll to the bottom of the app window in the dock > Tap on the device icon. The array of devices registered to your Amazon account will be displayed > Select the Amazon Echo dot device since it is the device you are returning to its factory default > Go to the button of the list of options in the Device settings > Select Deregister > You will then be asked to actually confirm your selection afterward.

It is to be noted that when a blue indicator appears, this shows that the device is undergoing the factory reset process, which will spin for approximately one minute. Immediately after the factory reset process is concluded, a message saying "Hello, to continue, download the Alexa app" will be played by your device. This will come in a different language.

Once you get this message, it implies that your device has been deregistered from the Amazon account and undergone the factory reset process.

How to Mount your Amazon Echo Dot 3rd Generation

Mounting your Echo dot provides you with the possibility of sticking your device to the wall without the use of screws though the Echo Dot comes with screws. Being able to mount the Echo dot eliminates the use of screw-in positioning it.

The whole free Total mount for the Echo dot comes in two different colors, which are the White and the Black. Other components that come with the free mount are some screws, a sticky tape as well as a thank you card.

Sticky tape: The Sticky tape helps you in quickly mounting it on the wall at your convenience. It is placed at the back of the mount so that whenever you want to mount it, all you will need to do is to pull off the backside and place or stick it anywhere you want it to be placed on the wall. You can then mount your echo dot device and get it plugged.

The sticky tapes will help in preventing your walls from being destroyed while providing you with the convenience of mounting your device and removing it whenever you want to.

Components that come with your TotalMount includes the following:

i. Screws that are used for mounting to the wall.

ii. A thank you card.

iii. A mount for your Amazon Echo dot unit: The Amazon echo dot mount is made from durable plastic as well as a ring that helps in keeping or hiding your wires. A pinhole is also available to assist in screwing it to your outlet in your office or home. At this point, what that is needed to be done is plugging it to the back.

Real-time installation of your Amazon echo dot

To install your Amazon echo dot using the TotalMount, take the following steps:

i. Detach the screw in the center of the plate and have it aligned to the holder.

ii. Fix the longer screw to the center and get it screwed.

iii. Plug into your power supply afterward.

iv. Put the cord outside the frame and place the cover.

v. Plug the Echo Dot unit and you can get started.

How to use the Echo dot with the Apple Music

The Echo dot of the 3rd generation has also been designed to work with the Apple music just like the Amazon Music, Spotify, Pandora, etc. Now you can also use Alexa commands to call up your playlists made on the Apple music with ease.

To play your Apple Music on the Echo device, you will need to have the Apple Music membership and get the Skill log downloaded into your account. It's advisable to have your Apple music set to default so that whenever you use the Alexa commands in getting music played; it will automatically play songs from the

Apple music. Once you have been able to add the Apple Music as your echo device, apart from being able to play across multi-room speaker groups throughout your home, you will also be able to do stuff like bringing up your playlist, calling up artists or songs you like to play, play radio stations as well as setting your alarm such that you will always wake up to your Apple music every morning.

Nevertheless, it also has its limitations, part of which is that you cannot add music to your playlist, and it will only give access to the primary account holders.

To get started setting up your Apple Music on your Echo dot device, take the following steps:

i. Get your smart device.

ii. Go to Skills & Games.

iii. Find Apple music and enable it.

iv. Log in to your account.

v. You will be asked with an option to make it your default music.

Once you have set the Apple music to default, you can start using the voice commands in getting songs played and also get to set the alarms to wake you up at a particular time to particular music such as "Echo, wake me up at 8:oo am to Bruno Mars." You can get to cancel the alarm by simply saying, "Echo, cancel alarm 8:oo am."

How Echo dot works with the Xbox one

The Echo dot 3rd generation work with the Xbox one using the Alexa voice assistant by Amazon. The first actionable step is to set up your Echo dot is super easy as earlier treated in the previous chapters.

To start, you will need to power your Echo dot device, and it also comes with a 3.5-millimeter port just in case you want to connect the device to an external speaker. To get started with linking your Xbox one, you will need to take the following steps:

i.Download the Alexa app. Once the Alexa app has been installed, you will be asked to set up your device, which is very easy once you are in.

ii. Go to Skills and search for the Skills you want or browse through the Skills that are already made available on the app. Since we are working on the Xbox, you will have the Xbox skill enabled.

iii. Once it is connected to your Xbox, you will be asked for your Microsoft account as well as a password with every other information needed.

iv. Afterward, you can go ahead and turn your Xbox on by using Alexa commands, such as "Alexa, turn on Xbox."

Once you have been able to follow these steps correctly, you will have absolute control over your Xbox using the Alexa commands.

How to Setup Amazon Echo dot 3rd Generation using Laptop

You don't need to access your mobile phone before setting up your Echo dot; you can get on your PC or laptop and access the Alexa on the Amazon web page.

i. Go to the settings and click on it.

ii. Then go ahead and click on the "Set up a new device" afterward.

iii. Click on the Echo dot.

iv. A notification will ask you to sign in to your Amazon account.

v. Then you will be prompted by a message which will say let's get you a code or connected to Wi-Fi.

vi. After this, press the button on the top of your Echo dot or any Amazon Alexa device you are using, we are concentrating on the Echo dot 3 here.

vii. You will press the dot button for 6 seconds, which will navigate you to the setup mode. Then you will have to follow the prompts in the Alexa app. The Echo dot will listen to you at this point to set that mode.

viii. Go back to your PC and go to your Wi-Fi devices list. The Amazon device should now be listed on your Wi-Fi device list and click on this to connect.

ix. Now go back to the Alexa app.

x. The next point of action is to go back to your computer, and you continue with the setup. You have to click continue and select whichever network you need to connect to your device.

xi. Make sure you link up to the same Wi-Fi network the echo dot is connected.

So this is how you connect your Alexa device with your laptop or your PC which is an effortless way to connect your echo dot to any Wi-Fi network through the PC.

How to Enable Echo Parental Controls

Parental control is a free option that can be easily enabled on your device. Amazon refers to this as Free Time for Alexa devices. You need to have the Alexa app downloaded on your Smartphone. If you are yet to get the app, you can easily get it from the Amazon App Store , Google playstore or from iTunes for it to work seamlessly.

Nevertheless, it is advisable to uninstall and install the app again from the Amazon App store even if you already have the app. This is because the Parental control features are brand new, and some of its features are still missing, notably in the Alexa app version that is provided by third-party app stores. To enable the parental control feature, you are required to take the following steps:

Go to the Alexa app > Tap on the Menu button at the top-left corner denoted by three horizontal lines > Tap "Alexa Devices" > A list will be displayed from which you will select your Echo device > Go to the "General" section . Select "FreeTime." > Next, to the "FreeTime" option, click on the Toggle > Parental permission will need to be provided here by entering your Amazon password as well as the verification passcode that will be sent to your phone > Select "Continue."

How to Play Spotify on the Alexa

Spotify is one of the top streaming music services, and the Alexa enabled speaker can be used to play music. Alexa can be asked to play songs, genres, artists, playlists, etc. To get Spotify connected to the Alexa, you are required to take the following steps:

Get the Spotify Premium account, which is subscribed at $9.99 per month. An Alexa speaker that can stream Spotify will also be needed, and thankfully, your new Amazon Echo dot of the third generation can do that. It's important to note that not all Alexa-enabled speakers can do this.

The second step is to have your Spotify account linked to the Alexa and set it as your default music service.

i. Go to the Alexa app.

ii. Select "Settings" at the left-hand menu, which is denoted by three horizontal bars.

iii. At the Alexa Preferences subheadings, select "Music & Media."

iv. Select "Link account on Spotify.com."

 v. Select "Log in to Spotify" on the next screen that is displayed.

 vi. You will then be prompted to log in using your Facebook credentials or Spotify account.

vii. Select "OKAY."

Once you select OKAY, you will be notified that your Spotify account has been paired correctly > Press x at the upper-right corner > Navigate back to the Media and Music tab of the Alexa settings menu. You will see that your Spotify has been linked having your account name just below the Spotify logo > Select "Choose Default Music Services." > Choose Spotify from the Default Music Library section > Scroll down and select "Done."

Once you have been able to follow all these steps correctly, anytime you ask Alexa to play music, it will automatically go into your Spotify and play the music. The Alexa can be asked to play specific songs, artists, playlists, and genre of music. The Alexa will only play music from a different source if you specify it should do so when saying the Alexa commands. You can as well perform other actions like increasing or decreasing your volume, skip to the next track, repeating songs, etc.

How to play your Spotify on Alexa through App

The Spotify app can be used in selecting which of your Alexa device you like to use in playing music. This can be done from your Mobile device or by making use of your tablet. You are required to take the following steps to do this:

Go to the bottom of the home screen > You will have the name of your current song displayed as well as available devices > Select "Devices Available." > A list of all the connected Alexa devices will be displayed, where you can select which one you like to play your music from.

How to Set Amazon Echo Alarm on the Echo Dot 3rd Generation

An alarm is a great feature that is available on the Alexa-enabled Echo dot generation devices, and there are several ways to set your alerts on these devices.

The easiest way to set Alarm on Alexa-enabled devices including the Echo dot 3rd generation is asking Alexa to wake you up at the 7 am and set the alarm with the default alarm sound. However, this can be easily changed in the Alexa app settings. You can also ask Alexa to set up a repeating alarm on your gadgets by asking her to get the Alarm set for every weekday.

The Alarm can also be set on the Alexa app on your Smartphone without having to use your voice in fixing it. This can be done by taking the following steps:

Go to the Alexa app on your Smartphone > Tap "Reminders and Alarms" on the left-side menu. Any alarm that was previously set will appear here > Select "Add Alarm," which will let you set the time, date, repeat settings, and the sound you would like to wake up to.

You can only set music alarms on Echo using the voice commands since the song can't be selected within the Alexa app's settings. There will be the need to inform Alexa about what song, playlist or artist you would like to wake up to in the morning by making sure your music service is appropriately set up within the Alexa app's settings.

How to Train Amazon Echo Dot 3rd Generation to recognize your voice

If your Amazon Echo dot often misunderstands your questions and commands, because you are staying in a place where you have multiple Amazon Echo users available, thereby making it difficult for Alexa to recognize who is speaking. The Alexa can be trained to recognize your voice whenever you talk by creating a voice profile. Anyone who is over 13 years old is eligible to create a personalized voice profile.

Once you can set up your voice profile, the Alexa will be able to call you by your name as well as deliver to you personalized results based on the recognition of your voice. It will be able to effectively differentiate your voice from that of the other people in your household. To do this, you are required to take the following steps:

Open the Alexa app on your Mobile device > Tap on the menu icon > Select Settings > Select Alexa Account > Select Recognized Voices.

Talk to Alexa by tapping "Voice." You will then be prompted by a welcome menu which will explain what the Voice profile is all about. It will tell you about how it enables Alexa to send and play messages as well as placing shopping orders without having to ask about who you are.

Slide to the lower part of the screen and select "Begin." > A prompt will then come up on the next screen with a message saying Alexa is now ready to get to know you. Do the following within five minutes of selecting the Begin button:

- Silence nearby devices.
- Ensure you are not in a noisy place.

- Make sure you are within 1 to 5 feet of your Echo and then say, "Alexa, learn my voice."

Repeat after Alexa. Alexa will ask you for your name and then ask you to speak ten phrases. Including phrases that will begin with Alexa's wake words such as Amazon, Computer, and Echo > As soon as you are done repeating the phrases, Alexa will inform you that it is nice to meet you and will suggest that you ask her to do something to try out your new voice profile such as send a message, make a call or play music.

How to add another voice after adding the first Recognized voice on your Echo dot 3

To add another voice presumably another member of your family, they will need to sign in to the Alexa app through their mobile device or log yours out of your Mobile gadget and log back in with theirs. They will then need to repeat the steps above. If any problems occur whereby the Alexa has a problem recognizing the person speaking, all you need to do is to get her corrected, and it will not happen again.

How to delete your Alexa's Voice profile on the Echo dot 3rd Generation

It is possible for you to get any voice you must record removed by taking the following steps:

Tap on the Menu denoted by a hamburger sign > Select "Settings." > Tap on "Alexa Account." > Tap on "Recognized Voices." > Select "Your voice." > Tap "Delete my voice."

How to help Alexa Recognize speakers

The "Your Voice" menu provides many other options. You can get exposed to more training sessions with Alexa by tapping on the "Learn my voice" option.

To train your Alexa more, you can play recorded phrases from someone who also has a voice profile already by tapping on the name of the person that must have uttered the phrase to enable Alexa to identify the speaker quickly.

To do this, you will have to take the following steps:

Select the Get started > Select "Begin" from the next screen that comes up and play the first phrase and then select the speaker name > Play the next phrase again, then select the speaker name and continue this with this screen till you are done > Select "Finish." > You will be prompted with the "Great job!" screen where you will have the option of exiting or listening to more phrases for additional training. If you choose to listen to more sentences, the Alexa app will take you through another set of recordings, and you can exit if you feel Alexa has finished recording all the voices you need to record.

After you are done, you can ask Alexa to get some tasks performed. If you have gone through all the steps correctly, it should be able to respond to you without having any difficulty with who is speaking. Alexa can be asked to play your messages, call someone, send a message, do some shopping, play music or flash briefings and with your voice profile correctly created; she will provide you with a comprehensive, personalized experience. Even if you had to switch to someone else's account, the Alexa voice assistant should be able to identify your voice. To be sure Alexa knows who you are, you can use the following command: "Alexa, who's profile is this?" or "Alexa, who am I?"

How to Add an Amazon Echo Sub and Configure Alexa EQ settings on your Echo Dot 3 Generation

The Amazon Echo sub can be referred to as an individual gadget that helps in adding some nice earthy sound to your other Amazon gadgets. The Amazon Echo sub can be added the same way a speaker is added. If you are adding the speaker for the first time, Alexa will guide you through the process of pairing with another Echo speaker or a stereo pair. If you have already created a stereo pair before, you will have to delete the pairing first.

This compendium will be showing you how to get the Echo sub added manually. It is to be noted that only the Echo second generation, Echo dot third generation as well as either of the generations of Echo Plus can be used as a stereo when paired with the Sub.

Once you feel your Echo devices need more bass to play, you can be sure of the Echo sub as a reliable solution which is a dedicated subwoofer improving the sound quality of your music.

To create a speaker group with the sub, you will need to take the following steps:

Open the Alexa app > Go to the bottom right of the screen and tap the Control icon > A menu will appear from which you will tap on the Plus icon > Select "Add the Subwoofer/ Stereo choice.

Go through the instructions to make sure your speakers are in the correct configuration to be paired and tap on the continue icon.

To make a selection of speakers to be used:

- A list of your Echo audio output speakers will be displayed from which you can click first on the Echo Sub.

- The list that comes up will be changed, and you will be presented with the speakers that are compatible with the Sub from where you can select one or two speakers.

- It is to be noted that the latter will create a stereo pair and will only work if you select two speakers of the same type out of the list.

- Select "Next," which will have the speaker group created.

To manage your Alexa EQ settings:

The sound of your speakers can be effectively adjusted by making use of the EQ settings.

Go to the Alexa App > Go to the bottom right and select the Control icon > Tap "Echo & Alexa." > Select one out of the Echo speakers, which is in the speaker group, including the Sub > Go to the "General" option > Select "Sound." > Tap on Equaliser under Media. With the slider, you will get to increase or decrease the Midrange, Bass as well as the Treble > Tap on the back arrow when done. Changes will apply to all speakers in the group.

To delete the sub pairing:

The Sub pairing needs to be removed before getting to attach the Echo sub to a different product, and this can be done by taking the following steps:

Go to the Alexa app > Select the Control icon at the bottom right > Scroll to the lower part of the page and select your speaker group > Select "Delete Speaker set."

CHAPTER FOUR

TROUBLESHOOTING COMMON ECHO DOT 3RD GENERATION PROBLEMS

ISSUE: Wi-Fi Connection inconsistent or non-existent

The power always indicates the connectivity status of the Echo device LED that is placed on the bottom rear of the device. When the LED indicates a white color, it means that the Wi-Fi connection is good and working while the orange color indicates that there is no Wi-Fi connection. In a situation, you are having an issue with your Wi-Fi connection with your Amazon Echo dot device; here are a few things that you can try:

• Reboot the router then turn off your Echo device and turn on again.

• If this doesn't work and the network is observed to be fine anyway, it is advisable to have your Echo device repositioned away from nearby devices as they may be interfering with network signals.

• Another possibility is to decongest your Wi-Fi network by removing devices that are not in use from the network.

• You can as well try toggling between the 2.4GHz frequency to the 5GHz frequency or the other way round. Using the 5GHz will reduce interference, a stable connection, and it is usually less congested. For the 2.4GHz frequency, it works better with devices that are farther away from the router, especially when there is wall interference.

• You can also try moving your Echo device to higher ground, such as a bookshelf to help protect your Echo device from interference.

ISSUE: Alexa failing to connect to other devices

The Alexa is also good at acting as a voice-controlled smart home hub for a wide range of devices such as Honeywell, Wink, Philips, etc. Though discovering and connection can be their downside at times. To help solve this issue when it arises, you can try the following:

• Check to be sure your device is compatible with the Echo as they may sometimes need a bridge as we have in the Wink and SmartThings hub.

• You can as well rely on the IFTTT that is if this then that to help in bridging the compatibility gaps. You can also visit the IFTTT channel to guide you through.

• Follow the set-up instructions available for the smart home device before telling Alexa to discover it, and you may as well need to download a companion app.

• Also, make sure that the smart home devices, as well as your Echo device, are connected to the same Wi-Fi network.

• Check to ensure that you have the most recent firmware and software updates downloaded for your devices. Also, make sure that the skill of your smart home devices is all enabled in the Alexa app.

ISSUE: Alexa finding it difficult to understand you

When Alexa finds it difficult to understand your question, it may reply to you by saying, "I'm sorry, I don't understand the question." This is Alexa's most uttered phrase and can be annoying. For the Alexa to comprehensively recognize your voice, it will do so naturally, but there are ways you can avoid the issue of trying to repeat yourself all the time.

• Using the voice training tool is an excellent tool to help solve this issue. You can do this by visiting the Settings and then navigate to the vocal training in your Alexa app where you will be asked to speak 25 installed words or phrases to assist Alexa with getting used to your voice.

• You should then check with what Alexa heard afterward. It is to be noted Alexa keeps a record of all your requests, so that way you can view precisely what she heard. You can actually confirm this by going to the Alexa app's settings and then selecting History. This way, you will be able to recognize common misheard words and then repeat them more clearly.

• Lastly, you should check with the positioning. Be sure your Alexa is not close to noisy appliances such as stereo, TV, dishwasher, etc. Then it is particularly noted by Amazon that baby monitors or microwaves do cause interference with Alexa, and it is noted that your Echo device should be kept at least 8-inches from the wall.

Other Books by the Author

The Essential Amazon Echo Show Complete Guide: The Beginners Guide for Amazon echo show and Amazon echo Show 5, Amazon Echo Dot with Alexa

Are you considering getting an Amazon Echo Show Device? The arrival of the echo show a few years ago revolutionized the way we communicate with devices around the home, mostly with Alexa installed. Do you want to know the traffic situation before leaving home in the morning? Listen to the news at any time of the day? Update your shopping list for the week? You can be rest assured that with Alexa on your Echo Show, whatever your task, it will be seamlessly handled, giving you more time on your hands to carry out other duties. Our fast-paced world makes for ease of access to our devices necessary at all times. The home is now fully integrated with smart devices that can be controlled remotely and with audio command via Alexa.

This is a guide meant for beginners and geeks alike who know their way around any device. With the simple language in which the book is written, you are guaranteed of getting all that you need to form your new device. With the Echo Show, you can continuously upgrade your skill levels to integrate it more into your daily activities. With Alexa fully integrated into the Echo Show device of your choice, you will readily learn;

- How to set up your device

- Tips and tricks on how to enable skills

- How to watch movies, play music, etc.

- How to make and receive calls

- Fully use Alexa

- How to make use of the varying types of

- Echo Show devices available

- How to remotely set up the security camera

- How to make use of the thermostat

- How to troubleshoot your device

- Set up your daily schedule

- Getting familiarized and understanding your device is just a few minutes away.

You should have total control over your Echo Show and have it run the way it is meant to. Get your copy of "The Essential Amazon Echo Show Complete Guide; The Beginners Guide for Amazon echo show, and Amazon Echo Show 5, Amazon Echo Dot with Alexa" today.

https://www.amazon.com/dp/B07V1LQ8LT

The Complete Amazon Fire TV Edition with Dolby Manual: The Beginners User Guide, Tips and Tricks with Troubleshooting

With the newly launched "Amazon Fire TV edition with Dolby" it is imperative to have substantial knowledge of "What is" and "What's not." This is because getting this product will give you great value for your money, take my words for it!

This book has been able to concisely lay out the "most" essential tips and tricks for every beginner to get along with the new product with so much ease and less stress, I can assure you of this.

You will thereby be well equipped to maximize the POTENTIAL of this amazing latest product from the desk of the Amazon. Are you just planning to make a purchase and wondering, "WHAT'S NEW IN THIS YET ANOTHER AMAZON NEW FIRE TV DEVICE INTEGRATED WITH THE POPULAR DOLBY." Wouldn't you rather use a well-detailed USER GUIDE FOR BEGINNERS WITH ALL THE TIPS AND TRICKS TO GET FAMILIAR FOREVER instead of wasting valuable time and energy trying to figure out how to RUN THE INITIAL SET UP?

WHAT EXACTLY IS THE AMAZON FIRE TV ALL ABOUT AND WHAT'S SO SPECIAL ABOUT THEIR INTEGRATION WITH DOLBY? All these are questions answered in this book, and perhaps you might as well already have an idea about the two giant companies, AMAZON and DOLBY. But do you know what; the lovely ALEXA FEATURES are still being maintained in this new device from Amazon? GOOD TO HEAR, ISN'T IT?

THE GREAT VOICE ASSISTANT, ALEXA AND HOW TO MAKE USE OF IT IS CONCISELY EXPLAINED HERE!

ARE YOU AWARE YOU CAN USE THIS DEVICE WITH YOUR KIDS WITHOUT GETTING WORRIED ABOUT WHAT THEY VIEW WHEN AWAY? YES, YOU CAN, THE USE OF THE PARENTAL CONTROLS EXPLAINED CONCISELY HERE WILL HELP YOU MAINTAIN A BALANCE KEEPING EVERYONE HAPPY.

You are a click away from finding all the answers to many questions you might have. You will also be embraced in this book with simplified tips and tricks to:

• Set up your new Fire TV edition with Dolby

• Get the necessary knowledge to start using the Alexa

• Get information on how to make use of the Parental controls

•   Install critical Apps of your choice

• Get your new Fire TV paired with other echo devices

• Improve the privacy needed on your device; guess everyone needs some privacy at certain times anyway.

•   Keeping up with your Fire OS updates

• Getting live TV configured on your device

•   Enabling the Fire TV remotes

•   Effectively managing your TV

• Viewing local content on your Fire TV

• Repairing your Fire TV Remote

•   Many   more

Get all these and so much more! SCROLL UP AND CLICK THE BUY NOW BUTTON TO GEET YOUR COPY OF THIS AMAZING BOOK NOW!

<u>https://www.amazon.com/dp/B07V332KFV</u>

The Kindle Fire 7, Fire HD 8 and Fire HD 10 with Alexa Complete User Guide: A Step by Step Guide to Troubleshoot, Tips and Tricks, Master your Device in 60 Minutes or Less!

The Kindle Fire HD ranges of tablets are some of the best gadgets that you ever get. It is worth every penny with the excellent build, OS, and amazing features that come with it to keep you entertained all day long. Whatever you have in mind from reading to watching movies, listening to music to turning it into a hub for the smart devices in your home, the list is just endless with what you can do with your Kindle Fire HD Tablet. These tablets are in a class all by themselves, and no other tablet comes close.

This guide is for everyone from tech-savvy folks to beginners. Getting your head around the plethora of features on the HD tablets can be a mind-boggling experience, and if you are not aware of the existence of such features, you will be grossly underutilizing the powers of your gadget. This book will give you a step by step tour on unraveling the mysteries that lie beneath the hood of your device. You will learn how to set up, personalize, maximize, and troubleshoot, and so much more. Here are some of the tips and tricks that you will learn;

- How to set up profiles Parental control features
- How to install Google Play on your device
- Load apps from other sources

- How to print books from your Kindle Fire HD

- Sharing books

- How to send mails

- How to make use of Alexa on your device.

This book is a must get for everyone. Click BUY and get started with your Kindle Fire HD Tablets today.

https://www.amazon.com/dp/B07V343BLQ

The Essential Amazon Fire TV Stick User Guide for Beginners: Simple Steps to Set Up Fire Stick, Connect Alexa, Add Video Streaming Apps, and Troubleshooting

Experiencing the fantastic audiovisual entertainment package in your Fire Stick device goes a step further than just scrolling through and clicking on shows or music tabs. It is a lifestyle that separates you from just about everyone else. This guide is the first step you take after getting the device to give you the basics about getting your Fire Stick Set up and essential tips on how to maximize the potentials of your device. Since it first graced our homes, the Fire Stick has been a must-have for techies and noobs alike. There are no more cable clutters all around your multimedia set up and with more recent advancements; the Alexa has been incorporated into this superb piece of technology, thereby making it simply awesome! The Fire Stick with its dynamic range of functions, is also quite easy to use, and you can be streaming great shows and games within a few minutes of unboxing your device. Getting this book will grant your powers of controlling your Fire Stick to levels you never knew existed.

You will get to learn the following and much more by getting this book:

-   Setting up your Fire Stick like a pro
-   Set up and connect Alexa and make use of audio activated commands
-   How to navigate the user interface
-   Connecting the device to the internet
-   How to set up the connection of the device to your Amazon account
-   Set up Kodi and other video streaming apps
-   Troubleshooting, and so much more!

What are you waiting for? Click the BUY button immediately and get started with the world of the Fire Stick!

https://www.amazon.com/dp/B07S7SCXK5

The Ultimate Fire TV Cube Beginners User Manual: A Step by Step Guide to Set Up, Use Alexa Voice Control, Kodi and Troubleshooting

This book was written with the everyday person in mind. It is effortless to grasp the terms and get the best out of your Five Tv Cube. If you have just gotten delivery of your brand new Cube and are at a loss on how to maximize it, this book will get you started with that. Of what essence will it be if you have gotten such a top-notch device and don't know how to find your way around it? Worry not! Within the pages of this book, you will get very simple, non-techie ways of enjoying the array of entertainment on offer for you to enjoy. This book will guide you on how to:
- Unbox and set up the Amazon Fire Tv Cube

- How to make use of Alexa with your Tv Cube

- Controlling your gadgets at home with the Cube

- Operating the device with Satellite or Cable

- Installing Kodi and other streaming apps

- The best VPN to use Streaming tips and tricks

- How to enjoy and get the best out of your Amazon Fire Tv Cube Troubleshooting.

And so much more!

Click the BUY button and get started on this fantastic journey!

https://www.amazon.com/dp/B07S6Q91YF

About the Author

Clayton M. Rines is a techie who lives in and around gadgets. Knowing what makes devices all around us tick is his life ambition, and he is always on the lookout for new ideas to everyday technological problems. Bringing solutions to your gadget issues, giving opinions and tips on how to get the best out of your devices, and bringing to you excellent news gives him so much pleasure. He is DIY expert, naturalist and animal lover.

Clayton is from Sacramento, California and enjoys globetrotting, savoring new experiences, enjoying new cultures.

CPSIA information can be obtained
at www.ICGtesting.com
Printed in the USA
LVHW050942261122
734073LV00004B/438